SCHOLASTIC discover more™

weather

By Penelope Arlon
and Tory Gordon-Harris

Free digital book

You can be a weather forecaster! Your digital book is packed with experiments and projects to help you observe, track, and predict weather.

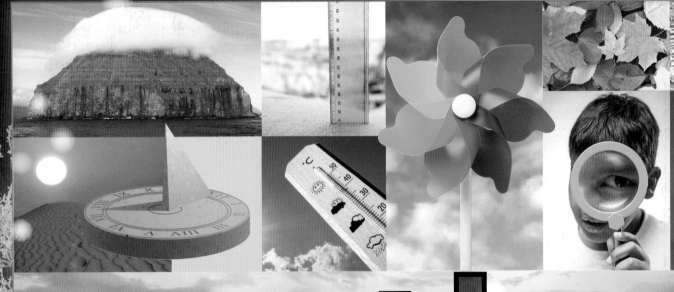

weather
watcher

A digital companion to **Weather**

Download your all-new digital book,

Weather Watcher

Log on to
www.scholastic.com/discovermore

Enter this special code:

RCFPRDHFGFW4

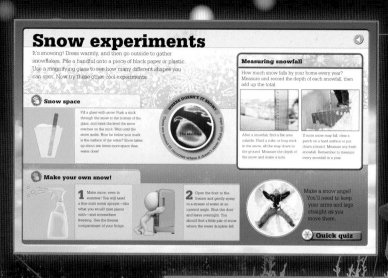

Snow experiments

It's snowing! Dress warmly, and then go outside to gather snowflakes. Pile a handful onto a piece of black paper or plastic. Use a magnifying glass to see how many different shapes you can spot. Now try these other cool experiments.

Snow space

Fill a glass with snow. Push a stick through the snow to the bottom of the glass, and mark the level the snow reaches on the stick. Wait until the snow melts. How far below your mark is the surface of the water? Snow takes up about ten times more space than water does!

Make your own snow!

1 Make snow, even in summer! You'll need a fine-mist water sprayer—like what you would mist plants with—and somewhere freezing. Use the freezer compartment of your fridge.

2 Open the door to the freezer and gently spray in a stream of water at an upward angle. Shut the door and leave overnight. You should find a little pile of snow where the water droplets fell.

Measuring snowfall

How much snow falls by your home every year? Measure and record the depth of each snowfall, then add up the total.

After a snowfall, find a flat area outside. Plant a ruler or long stick in the snow, all the way down to the ground. Measure the depth of the snow and make a note.

If more snow may fall, clear a patch on a hard surface or put down a board. Measure any fresh snowfall. Remember to measure every snowfall in a year.

Make a snow angel! You'll need to keep your arms and legs straight as you move them.

⊛ **Quick quiz**

Make great weather instruments: a barometer, a rain gauge, a sundial. Create weather in your kitchen, from snow to tornadoes.

hail larger than .. a baseball

Snow watch

HOME

How can you tell when it will snow? You can watch a weather forecast, of course, but you can also look for signs of snow yourself. The first place to look is the sky.

Predicting snow

Watch the clouds in winter. If the weather has been ice-cold and clear, and then you see thin sheets of streaky clouds high in the sky, snow may be on the way.

Check the temperature. If it has been very cold, below freezing, then the air warms up to about freezing (32°F / 0°C), the moisture in the air will increase. Then it will probably snow.

Powder snow is not very good for making snowballs; neither is hard, icy snow. Sticky snow is made up of larger snowflakes with lots of moisture—perfect for snowballs.

Snowflakes are made up of tiny **crystals** of ice. All snow crystals have six arms, or sides.

📷 **How to make snow**

⊛ **Snow on the ground**   ⊛ **Snow experiments**

Find fun, year-round activities for any kind of weather.

Snow on the ground

Look around your neighborhood on a snowy day for different kinds of snow. Some snowflakes trap more air between them as they settle; this affects the look and feel of snow, as do the temperature and the moisture in the air.

Powder snow

There is a lot of air trapped between the light, dry snowflakes of powder snow. This snow is ideal for skiing—but it isn't good for building, because the flakes of snow stay far from one another. Its **density** is less than 600 pounds for every 3.2 feet (200 kg/m) of snow

Compacted snow

There is very little space between the hardened flakes of compacted snow. It looks thin and icy rather than thick and soft, and it some sheets as it packs together. It's the kind of snow that you find on slopes or on slopes where people have been sledding all day!

Slush

After a snowfall, if the temperature rises or it rains, the snow melts and becomes slush. If the slush mixes with dirt, it turns gray or brown. Then, if the temperature drops again and the snow refreezes, the snow becomes icy and slippery.

Sticky with a crust

The wetter snowflakes are, the bigger and stickier they will become as more falling crystals stick to them. They form thick, sticky snow. If the top layer melts and then freezes solid again, it forms a hard, icy crust with soft snow underneath.

It's simple to get your digital book. Go to the website (see left), enter the code, and download the book. Make sure you open it using Adobe Reader.

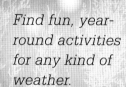

3

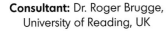

Consultant: Dr. Roger Brugge,
University of Reading, UK

Literacy Consultant: Barbara Russ,
21st Century Community Learning Center
Director for Winooski (Vermont) School District

Art Director: Bryn Walls

Designer: Ali Scrivens

Managing Editor: Miranda Smith

Managing Production Editor:
Stephanie Engel

US Editor: Esther Lin

Cover Designer: Neal Cobourne

DTP: John Goldsmid

Visual Content Project Manager:
Diane Allford-Trotman

**Executive Director of Photography,
Scholastic:** Steve Diamond

Library of Congress Cataloging-in-Publication
Data Available

ISBN 978-0-545-50516-1

10 9 8 7 6 5 4 3 2 1   13 14 15 16 17

Printed in Singapore   46
First edition, July 2013

Scholastic is constantly working to lessen the
environmental impact of our manufacturing
processes. To view our industry-leading
paper procurement policy, visit
www.scholastic.com/paperpolicy.

Contents

Our turbulent Earth

Our turbulent Earth

Our planet is frequently battered by
wild weather, caused by the movement of heat
and water in the atmosphere. Right this second,
there are about 1,800 thunderstorms in our skies.

What is weather?

Weather is what happens around us in the atmosphere. The air is always moving, bringing heat, cold, rain, sunshine, winds, fog, or snow.

What is climate?

An area's climate is the average weather that it receives. Meteorologists observe, track, and predict weather and climate.

hot ··

·· cold

POLAR CLIMATE

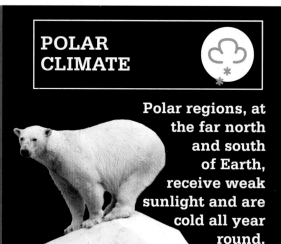

Polar regions, at the far north and south of Earth, receive weak sunlight and are cold all year round.

DESERT CLIMATE

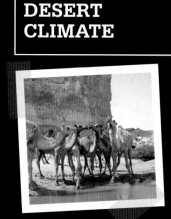

Deserts are areas that receive little or no rain. They may be hot, like the Sahara Desert, or cold, like the Gobi.

Water for life

Water covers 70 percent of Earth's surface. It rises into the atmosphere as water vapor and falls as rain or snow. Without this recycling of water, life on Earth could not exist.

Extreme weather

A turbulent encounter between heat and water can produce extreme weather, such as tornadoes. We are getting better at predicting extreme weather, but its effects can still be devastating (see pages 36–65).

TROPICAL CLIMATE

Areas near the Equator have tropical climates. The sunshine is strong, and it is warm most of the time. Some tropical areas also get a lot of rain.

TEMPERATE CLIMATE

Areas with temperate climates, like those in North America and Europe, have warm summers and cool winters.

Global warming

Many scientists think that humans are causing Earth to become warmer. This could have catastrophic effects on the weather and our lives.

Find out more about global warming on pages 72–73.

Earth's blanket

When you look up at the sky on a clear day, all the blue above you is the layers of the atmosphere—the blanket of gases wrapped around Earth.

The exosphere is the top layer of the atmosphere, which merges into space. The air here drifts away to almost nothing.

The thermosphere is also known as the upper atmosphere. It can get very cool at night, but direct sunlight can make it extremely hot near the top.

EXOSPHERE 375–6,200 mi. (600–10,000 km)

THERMOSPHERE 56–375 mi. (90–600 km)

MESOSPHERE 31–56 mi. (50–90 km)

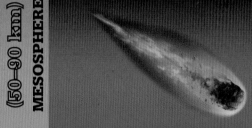

The mesosphere keeps meteorites from hitting Earth. The gases in the mesosphere cause the rocks to burn up.

STRATOSPHERE 12–31 mi. (20–50 km)

Airplanes may fly where the stratosphere is low to avoid bouncing around in the weather below.

TROPOSPHERE 0–12 mi. (0–20 km)

Most of the gas and water vapor in the atmosphere can be found in a dense layer just above the ground, called the troposphere.

Earth's atmosphere is 78% nitrogen, 21% oxygen, and

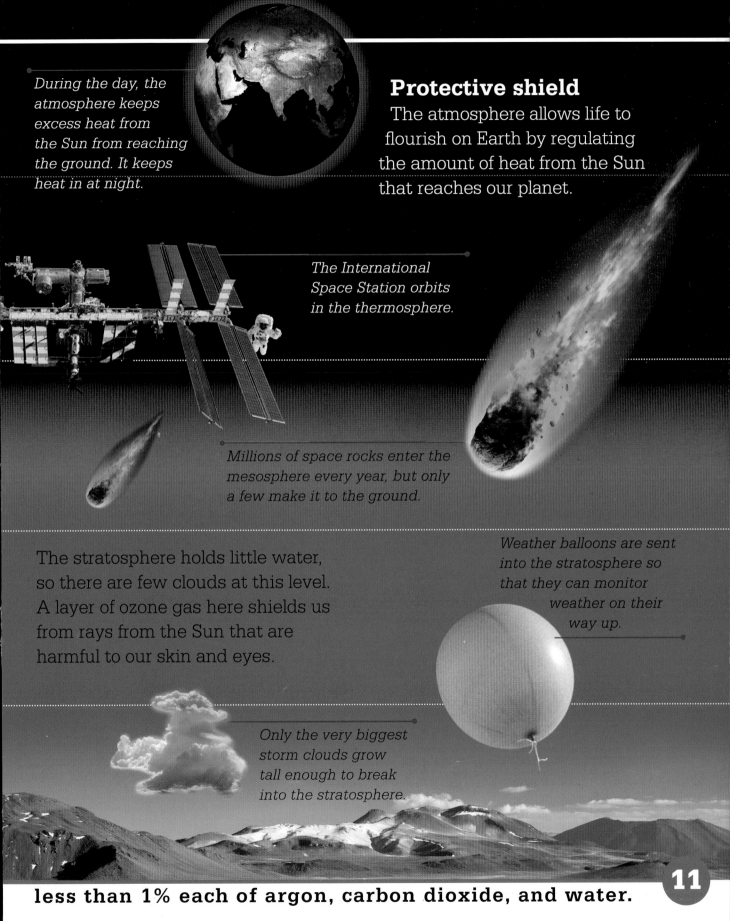

During the day, the atmosphere keeps excess heat from the Sun from reaching the ground. It keeps heat in at night.

Protective shield

The atmosphere allows life to flourish on Earth by regulating the amount of heat from the Sun that reaches our planet.

The International Space Station orbits in the thermosphere.

Millions of space rocks enter the mesosphere every year, but only a few make it to the ground.

The stratosphere holds little water, so there are few clouds at this level. A layer of ozone gas here shields us from rays from the Sun that are harmful to our skin and eyes.

Weather balloons are sent into the stratosphere so that they can monitor weather on their way up.

Only the very biggest storm clouds grow tall enough to break into the stratosphere.

less than 1% each of argon, carbon dioxide, and water.

Heat and wind

When the Sun is shining, it's often easy to forget that the weather is ever bad! In fact, heat from the Sun is responsible for all kinds of weather on Earth.

Traveling heat

The Sun's rays travel 93 million miles (150 million km) through space to heat Earth. Some areas on Earth receive more heat than others do; this causes the air to move.

Uneven heat

There are three basic reasons why some areas on Earth are hotter than others at any given time.

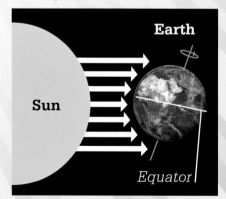

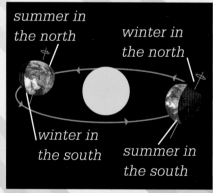

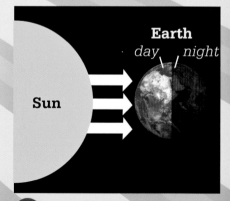

1 Round Earth

Earth's surface is curved, so sunlight shines directly on it at the Equator but hits the poles at an angle.

2 The seasons

Earth's tilt means that when the North Pole points toward the Sun, northern parts of the world get more sunlight.

3 Day and night

The Sun rises as Earth turns to bring each part of the world to face it. On the half of the planet not facing the Sun, it's night.

The movement of air on Earth causes wind, clouds,

Air movement

Hot air always rises, and cold air always sinks. When the air in one area is heated by the Sun and rises, cold air from a cooler area moves in to take its place. The air moves as wind.

HOT AIR RISES

COLD AIR SINKS

Air pressure

Air pressure is the weight of Earth's atmosphere pressing down on everything below it.

Cold air is more dense, and exerts high pressure.

Hot air is less dense, and exerts low pressure.

When you open the door from a warm house on a cold day, you can feel the cold air rushing inside the house toward you. That's wind, or air movement.

SUN FACTS

WHAT IS IT?
The Sun is a star. It is a ball of scorching hot gases.

HOW BIG IS IT?
About 1 million Earths could fit inside the Sun.

HOW HOT IS IT?
The Sun's core is 27 million °F (15 million °C). That's really hot!

HOW FAST IS LIGHT?
Earth is so far away from the Sun, it takes sunlight eight minutes to reach us.

storms, and all other weather   systems.

Dancing lights

Auroras

Magnetic bursts on the Sun may send streams of particles hurtling toward Earth. When they hit gas particles in the atmosphere, the impact creates waving colored lights, known as auroras. You can usually see them only near the North and South Poles.

Above, the aurora borealis, or the northern lights, fills

the sky over the mountains of Norway.

Measuring wind

How strong is the wind today? We describe wind using a scale that is hundreds of years old.

How fast?
An anemometer measures wind speed. The device's cups spin around in the wind, and their speed is measured in miles or kilometers per hour.

The Beaufort scale
In 1805, Sir Francis Beaufort of the British navy devised a scale and descriptions for wind speed.

At force 3, the wind extends small flags. Twigs and leaves on trees move.

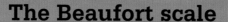

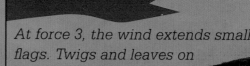

0 UNITS OF FORCE	1	2	3	4	5
calm	light air	light breeze	gentle breeze	moderate breeze	fresh breeze

At force 0, smoke rises vertically. The sea is calm.

At force 2, leaves rustle. Weather vanes begin to move.

At force 5, surface waves form on water. Small trees sway.

Winds are named for the directions from which they

Sea winds

At sea, there are no trees or buildings to slow wind down. The Beaufort scale was developed to warn ships about sea winds and is still used in shipping forecasts today.

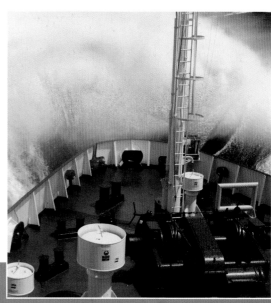

At force 6, trees begin to bend. Telephone wires whistle in the wind.

At force 12, there is great damage to structures on land. Waves grow to over 45 feet (14 m) at sea.

6	7	8	9	10	11	12
strong breeze	near gale	gale	strong gale	storm	violent storm	hurricane

At force 7, large trees move. Waves spray.

At force 9, there is some damage to houses. Waves are high.

At force 11, there is widespread damage on land and large waves at sea.

▶▶▶ Find out more ➤
about Earth's wind zones on pages 38–39.

arrive, so a southerly wind is blowing from the south.

Water cycle

The amount of water in the air stays constant. But that water is continuously recycled—lost as falling rain, then gained by evaporation.

2 The Sun's heat causes some of the surface water to evaporate, or turn into water vapor in the air. Watch a puddle disappear on a sunny day.

WATER COVERS 70% OF THE EARTH'S SURFACE.

1 Most of Earth's water is in oceans, rivers, lakes, and ice caps. Some seeps into the soil and is held underground before reemerging.

Water is held on Earth in three states: solid ice, liquid

3 As water vapor rises, it cools and condenses, or turns back into liquid and ice crystals. It is held in the sky as clouds.

4 If too much water condenses, the air can't hold it up. It falls back down to the ground as precipitation—rain, snow, or hail.

Rainbow

When it is sunny and rainy at the same time, sunlight may reflect off the water droplets, and you may see a rainbow.

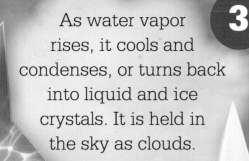

Dinosaur drink

Since all water is recycled, your next glass of water may have once been drunk by a dinosaur!

5 The water falls to Earth and flows downhill (or underground) until it joins a large body of water. The flow of land water to the ocean is called runoff.

water, and a gas called water vapor.

Light tricks

The white light from the Sun is actually a mix of colors that are scattered when the light hits water, dust, or ice crystals in the atmosphere. This phenomenon can produce some stunning light shows.

Seeing a rainbow

On days when it is both sunny and rainy, you may see a rainbow. A rainbow is formed when sunlight shines through raindrops. The white sunlight is broken into different colors that head in slightly different directions, so we see arcs of different colors.

Rainbow colors are always in the same order: red,

Other rainbows

Halo

A single colored ring around the Sun or Moon is called a halo. A halo appears when light splits into colors as it shines through ice crystals in high clouds.

Fog bow

When sunlight close to the ground breaks through fog, a pale or colorless arc called a fog bow may appear.

Double rainbow

Light may be reflected twice through a water droplet. This forms a bigger, fainter second rainbow, in which the order of colors is reversed.

orange, yellow, green, blue, indigo, violet.

Dew and frost

Even clear skies are full of water. On cool nights, it settles on the ground as dew and frost.

Morning dew

You can often see drops of dew sparkling on spiderwebs on chilly mornings. Dew forms when drops of water condense out of the air onto surfaces that have cooled in the night after a clear day.

Desert dew

Even in the desert, dew forms after a cool night. Dew has collected on this desert beetle, giving it an easy drink.

Frosty fog

When there is freezing fog or low-lying clouds, strong winds can freeze water drops onto trees. This hard "rime" ice turns the trees white.

Harsh frost can kill plants. They can withstand cold, but

Frost

Water vapor may freeze into white ice crystals, called frost, when the temperature is below freezing.

Fern frost

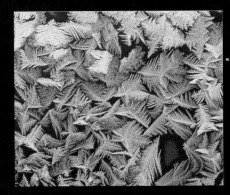

On very cold nights, dew may freeze into beautiful patterns on windows called fern frost.

Jack Frost

Jack Frost is a mischievous spirit from Viking folklore. Some say that he creates the frost on windows with his touch.

Small air bubbles trapped in the ice crystals give frost its white color.

Find out more ◀◀ about water vapor on pages 18–19.

the frosty ice crystals can damage their leaves.

Cloud spotting

You can be a cloud spotter! Learn to recognize different cloud types. Clouds are identified by appearance and height.

Cloud shapes

There are three basic cloud shapes. The ten most common clouds are combinations of these shapes.

Cirrus: 18,000–40,000 ft. (5,500–12,000 m)

Cirrocumulus: 20,000–40,000 ft. (6,000–12,000 m)

Cirrostratus: 18,000–40,000 ft. (5,500–12,000 m)

Altocumulus: 6,500–18,000 ft. (1,900–5,500 m)

Altostratus: 7,000–18,000 ft. (2,100–5,500 m)

Nimbostratus: 2,000–10,000 ft. (600–3,000 m)

Cumulus: 1,200–6,500 ft. (370–1,900 m)

Stratus: 0–6,500 ft. (0–1,900 m)

Winds blow clouds across the sky. High cirrus clouds

The three basic cloud shapes

1 Cirrus
These thin, wispy strands are often known as mares' tails.

2 Cumulus
These puffy clouds, like cotton balls, float alone or in clusters.

3 Stratus
A stratus cloud is a big white or gray sheet that fills the sky.

Cumulonimbus:
1,000–60,000 ft.
(300–18,000 m)

▶▶▶ **Find out more** about cumulonimbus storm clouds on pages 30–31.

Stratocumulus: 1,200–6,500 ft.
(370–1,900 m)

Fog
Fog is a very low-lying stratus cloud that hangs just above the ground.

Cloud names
The names of the ten most common clouds are made up of Latin words. *Cirrus* means "curl." *Cumulus* means "heap." *Stratus* means "spread out." *Altus* means "high." *Nimbus* means "cloud."

may travel at more than 100 mph (160 kph).

Cool clouds

You can spot strangely shaped clouds on most cloudy days. Look out especially for these, which are rare and spectacular.

NOCTILUCENT CLOUD
These rare clouds look like ocean waves. They sit high up in the sky and can be seen as the Sun sets.

SONIC BOOM CLOUD
When jets reach the speed of sound, they sometimes create their own clouds.

CLOUD OF LOVE
Look up at clouds for long enough, and you might see some weird and wonderful shapes!

Glider pilots "surf" morning

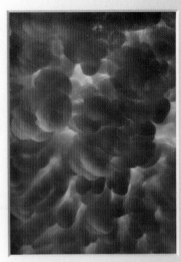

MAMMATUS CLOUD

These bulging clouds that droop from cumulonimbus clouds usually signal bad weather.

HOLE PUNCH CLOUD

When part of a cloud of water droplets freezes, this patch may fall, leaving a hole in the cloud.

JET CONTRAIL

Hot air from jet exhaust mixes with cold air, producing long trails of clouds across the sky.

MORNING GLORY CLOUD

Every spring, these clouds, some over 600 miles (970 km) long, sweep across northern Australia at up to 35 mph (55 kph).

LENTICULAR CLOUD

These clouds, created by wind blowing over mountains, look like flying saucers!

glory clouds, using the wind to speed themselves along.

Precipitation

Every day, more than 550 trillion tons of water falls to Earth as rain, snow, or hail. This water is known as precipitation.

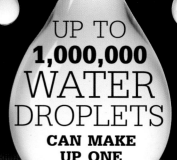

UP TO **1,000,000** WATER DROPLETS **CAN MAKE UP ONE RAINDROP.**

2 MPH

11 MPH

RAINY FACTS

SPEEDY RAIN
A typical snowflake falls at about 2 mph (3 kph); a raindrop falls at about 11 mph (18 kph).

RAINIEST VACATION
If you want a sunny vacation, then don't visit Mount Waialeale, on the Hawaiian island of Kauai. It rains about 350 days a year there.

BIGGEST FLAKE
The largest snowflakes ever recorded fell in the United States in 1877. They were 15 inches (38 cm) wide!

Torrential rainstorms
Cumulonimbus storm clouds can produce sudden, heavy rain that can swamp the area directly beneath it in a matter of minutes.

The most fatal hailstorm ever recorded killed 246

What is rain?

Tiny droplets and ice crystals in clouds may grow into big drops of water so heavy that they fall as rain.

What is snow?

If it's very cold, ice crystals may grow into snowflakes and fall as snow.

What is hail?

When ice crystals are lifted high in storm clouds, they are tossed around. They gain more layers of ice, then fall as hail.

All snowflakes have six arms, or sides. No two flakes are ever the same.

Giant hailstones

Hailstones the size of baseballs can fall from the sky during thunderstorms. They can fall at up to 100 miles per hour (160 kph) and may cause serious injury. The biggest hailstone on record was as big as a watermelon!

people in India on April 20, 1888.

Thunderstorms

There is nothing more awesome than a huge thunderstorm, with its fiery lightning and booming rumbles.

Storm clouds

When the air is especially warm and humid (damp), it rises and cools, building up huge cumulonimbus clouds. They grow taller and move around violently until they explode into thunder and lightning and fall as torrential rain.

STORM FACTS

BOMB CLOUD
One cumulonimbus cloud releases as much energy as a nuclear bomb does.

DEADLY STRIKES
Today, fewer than 30 people are killed by lightning strikes in the US each year.

STORM ABOVE!
Light travels so fast that we may see lightning before we hear thunder. But if a storm is overhead, thunder and lightning may arrive together.

What is thunder?

Thunder booms out when lightning flashes through the air. Lightning heats the air and makes it expand so fast that it sends out a shock wave of sound.

A rain-filled cumulonimbus cloud can weigh more

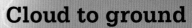

Lightning

Lightning begins inside a storm cloud. Ice crystals are torn apart and smashed back together, creating electricity.

Cloud to ground

The bottom of a storm cloud has a negative electrical charge, while the ground (and the cloud's top) is positively charged. Electricity leaps between the cloud and the ground in flashes—that's lightning!

What to do in a storm

Lightning takes the easiest route to the ground, so it will find the tallest object to strike.

DO NOT open your umbrella—lightning likes metal and will be drawn to it.

DO NOT jump in a pool. Lightning can strike water and may hit a solid object in it.

DO NOT stand under a tall tree. A direct strike can destroy even the toughest of trees.

DO stay indoors, but keep away from windows.

than 10,000 elephants. That's a lot of water!

Flashing skies

Forks of fire

Forked lightning flashes above Tucson, AZ. Each bolt heats the air to 54,000°F (30,000°C) for 0.2 seconds. That's five times hotter than the Sun's surface! The bolts can be up to 3 miles (5 km) long.

There can be as many as 100 lightning flashes in the

world every second. That's over 8 million a day.

Struck seven

Was Roy Sullivan the unluckiest man in the world—or the luckiest?

What are the odds?

The chance of being struck by lightning is very small. But the chance of being killed if you are struck is very high. Roy C. Sullivan defied the odds by being struck seven times . . . and surviving all seven strikes!

Sullivan was born in 1912 and started working as a park ranger in Shenandoah National Park, VA, in 1936.

year 1969

STRIKE TWO!

Sullivan was in his truck. Lightning hit a nearby tree and bounced through the truck's open window. The strike burned off his eyebrows, his eyelashes, and most of his hair.

year 1970

STRIKE THREE!

Sullivan was struck in his yard. The bolt hit an electric cable and jumped to his left shoulder, burning it.

year 1972

STRIKE FOUR!

Sullivan was inside the park ranger station. The lightning set his hair on fire, but he managed to put it out with a wet towel.

All seven strikes were confirmed by the chief ranger

1942

Strike one!

Sullivan was sheltering from a thunderstorm in a fire lookout tower. The tower was hit, and, as he described it, "fire was jumping around all over the place." He ran out, but not before lightning hit his toe, leaving a hole in his shoe.

Sullivan's wife was also struck once! She was hanging clothes in the yard, with Sullivan helping, but neither was harmed.

1973

STRIKE FIVE!

Sullivan left his truck in the park, thinking a storm was over—and he was struck once again! His hair was set on fire, and the bolt moved down his body and knocked off a shoe without untying the laces!

1976

STRIKE SIX!

This time, Sullivan was hit and injured on the ankle. He probably saw the thundercloud and tried to run away but was struck anyway.

1977

STRIKE SEVEN!

Sullivan was fishing when lightning hit the top of his head, singeing his hair. The bolt traveled down his body, burning his chest and stomach. When he turned around, a bear was eating the trout that Sullivan had caught— luckily, the bear left him alone!

of the park or by the doctors who treated him.

Extreme
weather

Extremes of heat, cold, wind, or rain endanger lives. Droughts are nature's biggest killer. People and animals may go without food and water, and no crops will grow. More than 10 million people in Africa alone may be at risk from droughts today.

Wind zones

Extreme weather can happen anywhere in the world, but some powerful winds always happen in the same places.

Trade winds

Winds just above the Equator blow toward it from a northeast direction; below the Equator, they blow toward it from the southeast. These nearly constant winds are called trade winds.

chinook

trade wind from the northeast

The flat plains of Tornado Alley, between two mountainous regions, provide perfect conditions for tornadoes.

Tornado Alley

Tornadoes can happen anywhere on Earth, but most occur in an area of the US Midwest known as Tornado Alley.

TORNADO ALLEY

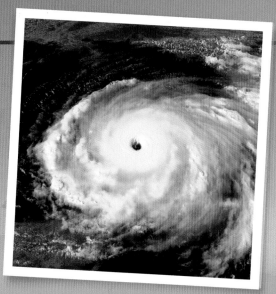

KEY TO MAP

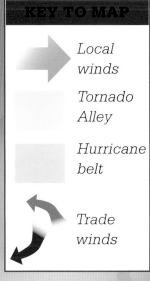

→ *Local winds*

☐ *Tornado Alley*

☐ *Hurricane belt*

↻ *Trade winds*

Hurricane belt

Tropical cyclones, or hurricanes, start over warm ocean waters near the Equator. They travel westward, in the direction of the trade winds.

mistral

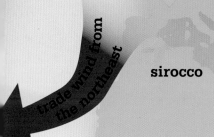

sirocco

trade wind from the northeast

Local winds

In many parts of the world, strong winds return at the same time of year. Local monsoon winds change direction with the seasons, often bringing heavy rain.

Indian monsoon

trade wind from the northeast

EQUATOR

trade wind from the southeast

Jet streams

Narrow, fast-moving streams of air high up in the atmosphere are called jet streams. They can help airplanes travel more quickly.

World War II. The winds blew pilots off course!

Twisting tornadoes

Tornado winds can spin at 300 mph (480 kph) and can

Twisters

Tornadoes are violent, whirling winds that are created during giant thunderstorms called supercells. They are the most powerful gusts on Earth. Tornadoes are usually about 250 feet (76 m) wide, but some have been up to 1 mile (1.5 km) across!

travel across the ground at 70 mph (110 kph),

Twister devastation

A tornado is the most violent weather that the atmosphere produces. It can pick up a house or train and break it into pieces. Three-quarters of all tornadoes happen in the United States.

TORNADO FACTS

HOW LONG DO TORNADOES LAST?

Most tornadoes last only about ten minutes, but some have traveled for several hours.

DO TORNADOES INJURE PEOPLE?

On average, tornadoes kill 70 people and injure 1,500 in the US each year.

WHEN WAS THE MOST DEVASTATING TORNADO?

In 1925, a single tornado hit three states, leaving a 219-mile (352 km) trail of destruction behind it. It killed 695 people.

Giant vacuum

Tornadoes don't just smash things, they pick up anything in their paths like vacuum cleaners—even cars and cows!

Enhanced Fujita scale

We measure a tornado's strength on the Enhanced Fujita scale.

Light damage *(breaks branches, chimneys)*

EF0

Moderate damage *(rips off roofs)*

EF1

When tornadoes roar across lakes or ponds, they have

How are they made?

Tornadoes begin in huge supercell storm clouds. They are often accompanied by thunder, lightning, hail, and very strong winds.

As warm air is sucked upward into a supercell, upper-level winds make it spin.

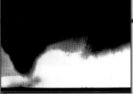

The rotating wind gathers force, and rain-cooled winds blow downward.

A funnel shape drops from the cloud, becoming a tornado as it hits the ground.

eye EYEWITNESS The terrible twisters of 2011

> I got back up and got hold of the door handle, and about that time the whole wall just went and opened to the outside and took me with it.

—Ken Carter, Apison, TN

Record-breaking season

In a single month, a record 758 tornadoes hit Tornado Alley.

Considerable damage *(derails trains)*

Severe damage *(flips cars over)*

Devastating damage *(lifts buildings, cars)*

Incredible damage *(hurls cars, destroys most things in its path)*

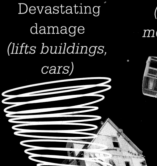

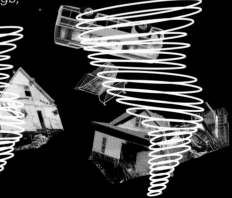

EF2   **EF3**   **EF4**   **EF5**

been known to pick up frogs, fish, and crabs!

Interview with a

Name: Sean Casey

Profession: Storm chaser, Tornado Intercept Vehicle (TIV-2) designer, IMAX filmmaker

Q **Have you always been interested in tornadoes? What was your greatest success?**

A I fell in love with them the first time I chased one, back in 1999. My greatest success was an intercept in 2009, when we took a direct hit in Goshen County, WY, while collecting data on the tornado's lower-level winds.

The filming turret can turn 360 degrees.

Q **Do you feel safe inside your TIV-2?**

A I only feel safe when it's stationary!

The heavily armored TIV-2 is designed to withstand powerful tornado winds so that it can film and take useful measurements.

Tornado chasing is dangerous, even for the experts.

storm chaser

Q **Have you been inside a tornado? Were you scared or excited?**

A I've been inside the circulation of 12 tornadoes. I felt both excited at being close to such an incredible force of nature but also terrified of what could happen.

Q **What does a tornado sound like?**

A Every tornado sounds different. Some small ones sound like whistles, and large, powerful ones sound like a combination of a train and a waterfall.

The instrument mast takes meteorological measurements.

TIV-2

So NEVER chase a tornado yourself.

Howling hurricanes

Hurricanes (also known as tropical cyclones or typhoons) are gigantic, spinning superstorms that start over tropical seas.

Brewing hurricanes

A hurricane begins above warm ocean water and usually moves westward. It loses strength if it reaches land, but often not before it wreaks havoc along coastlines.

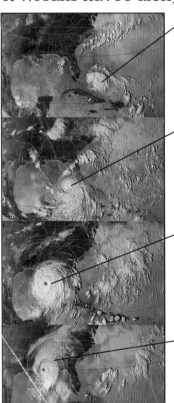

In 2005, Hurricane Katrina developed over the warm Atlantic Ocean.

As hot air rose, water evaporated from the ocean. A huge storm formed.

Earth's rotation made the clouds spiral around the eye, or center.

Katrina hit land, devastating New Orleans, LA, then lost strength.

Into the storm

Satellites can watch a hurricane, but the most accurate method of predicting its path is to fly straight into it, taking measurements along the way. It's a dangerous job, but the information can save lives.

Find out more ◀◀◀ about hurricane paths on pages 38–39.

The moment a hurricane forms, it is given a name.

The Saffir-Simpson scale

There are five categories of hurricane.

1 Minimal hurricane
74–95 mph
(119–153 kph)

2 Moderate hurricane
96–110 mph
(154–177 kph)

3 Extensive hurricane
111–129 mph
(178–208 kph)

4 Extreme hurricane
130–156 mph
(209–251 kph)

5 Catastrophic hurricane
157+ mph
(252+ kph)

Hurricane Sandy

If a hurricane's winds are whirling at least 74 miles per hour (119 kph), it is categorized on the Saffir-Simpson scale. Hurricane Sandy, in 2012, was a Category 2 storm at its worst.

Hurricane Sandy was enormous— it was 1,100 miles (1,770 km) wide!

Sandy's winds were strongest around the eye. But the center of the eye is normally calm.

47

The first of the season begins with *A*, then *B*, *C*, etc.

Hurricane Sandy

In October 2012, Hurricane Sandy began a path of destruction across the Caribbean and the US. It was to be the largest Atlantic hurricane on record.

The storm surge
As the hurricane reached the East Coast, it produced a storm surge that flooded much of the coastline.

Time line of Sandy in New York

While still Category 1, Sandy combined with another storm and became an incredibly rare superstorm.

Emergency food was brought into city hospitals.

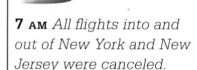
7 AM *All flights into and out of New York and New Jersey were canceled.*

Oct. 28, 2012

Oct. 29, 2012

7 PM *For only the second time in its 108-year history, the New York City train system was shut down.*

← 22-51
WALL ST

9:30 AM *As Sandy changed course and headed for the city, the New York Stock Exchange did not open.*

Over 8 million homes in the United States lost power

EYEWITNESS Hurricane Sandy hits

A home destroyed

The storm surge flooded Stephen Chin's house in Breezy Point, NY. It drenched his home and destroyed many of his family's belongings.

> "The water went from ankle to knee deep in minutes. We knew we had to escape. We drove out into the rain and wind that was spreading the fires around us."
>
> —Stephen Chin, Breezy Point, NY

1 PM *Winds reached 90 mph (145 kph). The storm surge began.*

8:30 PM *Water poured into an electrical substation, and all of lower Manhattan plunged into darkness.*

Thousands homeless

Oct. 30, 2012

4 PM *All along the East Coast, waves crashed across beaches, destroying houses.*

9 PM *The biggest residential fire in New York in 100 years blazed in Breezy Point.*

20,000 911 calls were received per hour.

to Hurricane Sandy.

Droughts

If an area gets no rain, or it's hot and dry for a very long time, there may be a drought— which can be catastrophic.

Disaster

Droughts can last for years, but even a short, intense drought can cause widespread suffering. Without rain, crops and water resources fail, and people may starve or be forced to leave their homes.

The Sahel drought lasted more than **15 YEARS.**

DESERT FACTS

LONGEST DROUGHT

The Sahel region of Africa suffered a drought that lasted from the 1960s to the 1980s. About 4 million cows died.

THE DUST BOWL

During the 1930s, an extreme drought caused millions of acres of farmland on the plains of the southern US to turn to dust. Half a million people were left homeless.

SUPERTOUGH TREE

The acacia can survive drought conditions because it has long roots that can reach deep water.

Half the livestock **in Somalia died in the**

2010–2011 drought

Millions of Somalian people were forced from their homes when crops failed during a terrible drought.

> "It's so extreme. . . . We estimate that one-quarter of Somalia's 7.5 million people are now either internally displaced or living outside the country as refugees."

—**UN High Commissioner for Refugees spokesperson Melissa Fleming**

Charity help

Often, countries experiencing droughts do not have enough resources to solve the problem and must rely on aid from charities. Many charities do amazing work bringing water, food, and shelter to people.

Charities build water pumps to provide clean drinking water.

Bushfire!

Raging fire

After a period of drought, all it takes is a little spark to set the parched landscape on fire. As the hot air rises, cool air rushes in below, causing winds that blow the fires across the land. Australia has thousands of bushfires every year. Some occur naturally, but most are started by people, accidentally or on purpose.

Birds of prey brave the heat of the fires, waiting to

snatch small animals that race out to escape the flames

Dust storms

In hot, dry areas, warm air rises, and cool air may sweep downward to replace it, picking up loose dust or sand. Stay inside—it's a dust storm!

Volcanic weather

Volcanoes can affect weather. In 1980, Mount St. Helens in Washington threw ash 12 miles (19 km) into the sky. This caused hazy skies across the globe, and a brief drop in temperature.

Sandstorms

Powerful gusts in the desert can pick up huge amounts of sand, lifting it high in the sky. Winds carry the sand and dump it far away. It sometimes mixes with rain and falls as mud.

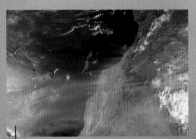

A Saharan sandstorm sweeps 1,000 miles (1,600 km) across western Africa, covering the Canary Islands.

The sand blots out the light of the Sun, casting a creepy yellow glow.

Wall of dust

A haboob is an intense dust storm that looks like a thick wall. This haboob in Sudan, Africa, is caused by a seasonal wind change. The storm can be 3,300 feet (1,000 m) high and move at 60 miles per hour (100 kph).

Dust devils are sometimes called dancing devils, or

Eyjafjallajökull

A huge volcano in Iceland erupted in 2010. A giant ash cloud spread and kept airplanes in Europe grounded for six days.

> "It was a bit scary, but still amazing to see. The ash had started falling and we couldn't leave the car."
>
> —**Katrin Moller Eiriksdottir, Fljotshlid, Iceland**

Dust devils

Dust devils are spiraling columns of dust that can move across the ground and grow to 1.2 miles (2 km) high. They occur if the ground is hotter than its surroundings, causing air to rise very quickly and pick up dust.

willy-willies in Australia.

Harsh climates

People live on almost every landmass on Earth. They have adapted to exist in extreme and dangerous climates.

El Niño

Every few years, the Pacific Ocean heats up and warm water moves east, causing weather changes. South America receives strong rains and floods; Australia may suffer droughts.

Windiest city

The city of Wellington lies in a "wind corridor" between the two islands of New Zealand.

EXTREME PLACES

COLDEST PLACE ON EARTH

The lowest recorded temperature was −128.6°F (−89.2°C), at the Vostok Research Station in Antarctica in 1983.

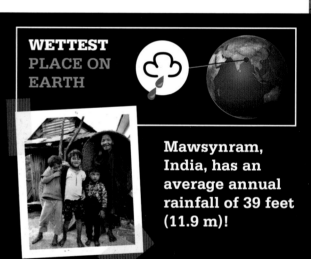

WETTEST PLACE ON EARTH

Mawsynram, India, has an average annual rainfall of 39 feet (11.9 m)!

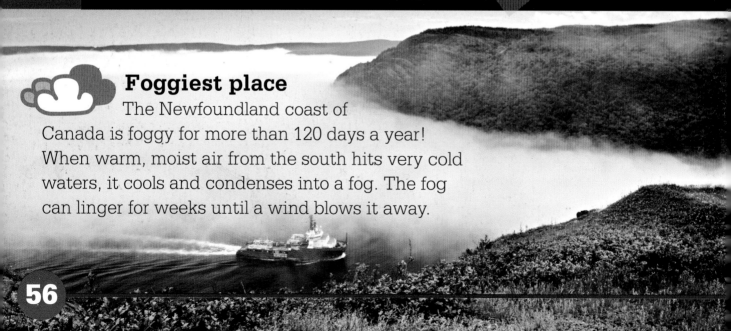

Foggiest place

The Newfoundland coast of Canada is foggy for more than 120 days a year! When warm, moist air from the south hits very cold waters, it cools and condenses into a fog. The fog can linger for weeks until a wind blows it away.

Hottest inhabited place

Temperatures in the Danakil Desert, Ethiopia, can average over 93°F (34°C), day and night. At mid-afternoon, it averages 104°F (40°C)!

The Afar people of the Danakil Desert eat mostly meat and milk, since it is difficult to grow crops in the desert.

WORST HIT BY
TROPICAL CYCLONES

The islands of the Philippines, in Southeast Asia, can be hit by up to 20 tropical cyclones in a single season.

DRIEST
PLACE ON EARTH

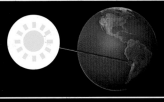

Some areas of the Atacama Desert, in South America, once didn't get any rain for 400 years!

Coldest town

Verkhoyansk, Russia, is one of the coldest inhabited places in the world. Winter temperatures average –49°F (–45°C).

The Yakut people live in Verkhoyansk. They wear reindeer skins to keep warm.

It is so cold there that when you exhale, your breath freezes into ice and falls to the ground!

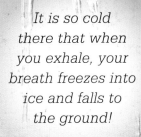

Floods

Floods cause more damage and deaths than any other weather. Bangladesh, in Asia, is one of the most flooded places in the world.

Monsoon winds

A monsoon is a wind that changes direction seasonally, causing wet and dry seasons. The summer monsoon brings heavy rainfall.

Bangladesh

Every year, Bangladesh floods during the three-month monsoon season. About 90 percent of the annual rain falls at this time.

IN **1998**, THE FLOODS IN BANGLADESH LEFT **30,000,000** PEOPLE HOMELESS.

FLOOD FACTS

YANGTZE FLOOD
In 1998, the Yangtze River in China flooded for three months, affecting 230 million people and killing over 3,500.

HURRICANE KATRINA
In 2005, Hurricane Katrina caused huge floods in New Orleans, LA. Over 1,800 people died.

BANGLADESH
In 1998, 70 percent of Bangladesh lay under floodwater.

Although floods cause damage, they also make the

India

Bangladesh

Indian Ocean

The monsoon sweeps in from the cold Indian Ocean to the warm land.

Bangladeshi floodplain

The torrential monsoon rains fill and break the banks of the Ganges River, flooding the flat land of Bangladesh.

Floods often leave people stranded, and their homes may be totally destroyed.

Getting to school

During floods, when roads are impossible to use, boats can transport people. School boats pick up children so that they do not miss too much school.

Flash floods

Flash floods happen when heavy rain falls on dry, hard ground and can't drain away. They can happen in minutes.

Arkansas, 2010

In the early morning of June 11, 2010, rivers in Arkansas rose over 20 feet (6 m). The water burst the riverbanks and swept over the land, killing 20 people.

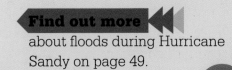

Find out more
about floods during Hurricane Sandy on page 49.

about floods during Hurricane Sandy on page 49.

soil much more fertile for growing crops.

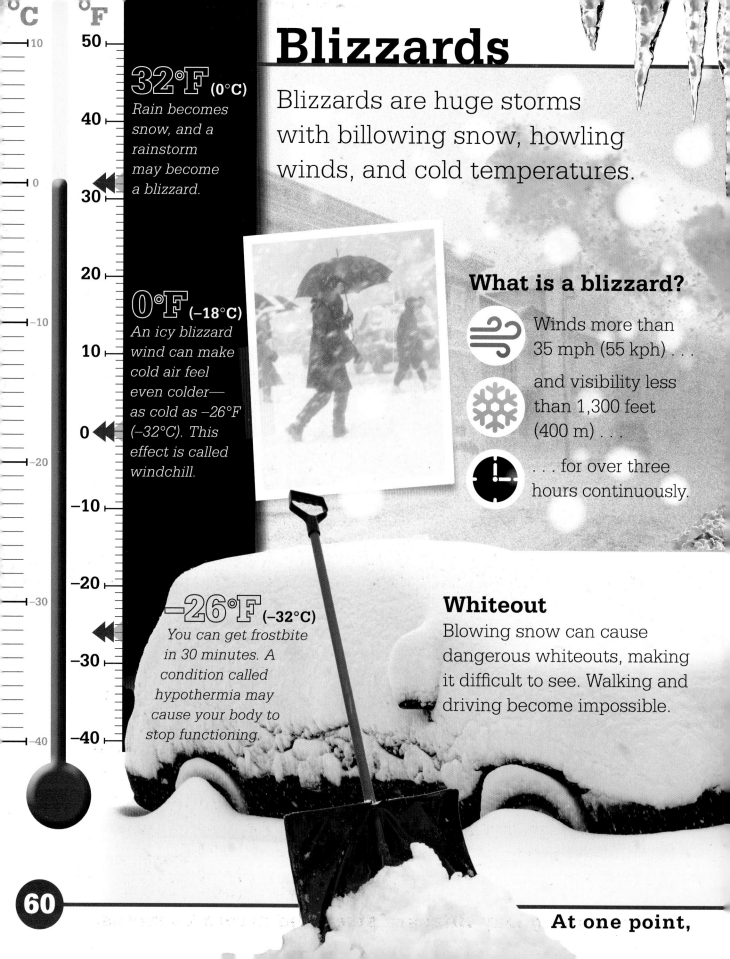

°C | °F

10
50

40
32°F (0°C)
Rain becomes snow, and a rainstorm may become a blizzard.

0
30

20
0°F (−18°C)
An icy blizzard wind can make cold air feel even colder— as cold as −26°F (−32°C). This effect is called windchill.

−10
10

0

−20
−10

−20
−26°F (−32°C)
You can get frostbite in 30 minutes. A condition called hypothermia may cause your body to stop functioning.

−30
−30

−40
−40

Blizzards

Blizzards are huge storms with billowing snow, howling winds, and cold temperatures.

What is a blizzard?

Winds more than 35 mph (55 kph) . . .

and visibility less than 1,300 feet (400 m) . . .

. . . for over three hours continuously.

Whiteout

Blowing snow can cause dangerous whiteouts, making it difficult to see. Walking and driving become impossible.

At one point,

Snowdrifts

Blizzard winds blow snow into drifts that can reach 40 feet (12 m) high. It can take snowplows days to clear the roads.

Three-day blizzard

Starting on January 31, 2011, a blizzard swept across North America. About 2 feet (60 cm) of snow fell on Chicago, IL.

> "It took us all night, but we got [50 people stuck in their cars] out. Most of these people didn't have good winter clothes, no gloves, no hats, no food or water. They weren't prepared."

—Dwain Stadie, **snowmobile rescuer, Illinois**

61

Weird weather

Weather can do some strange things. Sunlight can trick you into seeing eerie illusions. And yes, it can rain animals!

 hailstones

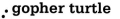 gopher turtle

It's hailing turtles!

In 1894, a severe hailstorm in Mississippi surprised residents when it dropped an ice-covered gopher turtle out of the sky!

Is it a ghost?

This uncanny figure is actually a weird version of your shadow. It can appear on a misty mountainside when the Sun is behind you—creepy!

Road sharks

In 2011, flood victims in Australia had to deal with another danger. Sharks were swimming up the flooded streets, right through town centers!

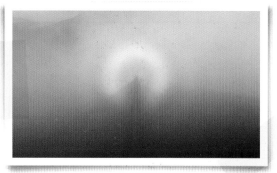

Why does it rain animals?

It is thought that animals are picked up in waterspouts or very strong winds, carried up to 60,000 feet (18,000 m) into the air, then dropped. But nobody knows for sure.

Imagine seeing blood rain! Storms sweep up red sand

How many Suns?

These mysterious triple Suns may be seen when the Sun is low in the sky in cold weather. It's a strange trick of the light!

In 2011, Scottish schoolchildren were pelted by a rainstorm of worms!

In 2010, Hungarians experienced a sudden downpour of frogs during a thunderstorm.

In 2010, hundreds of small fish fell from the sky over a town in Australia's Northern Territory.

Occasionally, frogs have survived the fall. Which suggests that they didn't travel far before being dropped.

Find out more ◀◀◀
about weird clouds on pages 26–27.

from deserts. The sand mixes with rain, turning it red.

Our weathered planet

Weathering

Wind and rain can wear down and move rock and soil in a process called erosion. Leftover rock may be strangely shaped, like the Queen's Head rock in Taiwan.

Hoodoos

Melting snow collects in cracks in rock. It freezes and expands on cold nights, then thaws. Over time, the rock may break and reshape. This process created these hoodoos in Utah.

Wave rock

This 46-foot-high (14 m) cliff in Hyden, Australia, was shaped by chemicals dissolved in rainwater, which softened the rock in a unique way.

Stone forest

The Grand Tsingy landscape in Madagascar is the world's largest stone "forest." The rocks were eroded by natural chemicals in the tropical rain. They are up to 300 feet (91 m) tall.

Some Native Americans believe that hoodoos are

Fairy chimneys

Over centuries, wind and rain eroded rock into pillars in Cappadocia, Turkey. Long-ago people made them into houses and churches, and decorated them.

Chocolate hills

Rainwater and underground water slowly dissolve limestone rock. In Bohol, the Philippines, this process created 1,500 cones— the chocolate hills.

Balanced rock

Although this rock, in Yorkshire, UK, looks like it is just about to topple over, it has actually been there for tens of thousands of years, eroded by rain and ice.

Swirling rock

Strong winds can erode rock and move soil. Over thousands of years, wind erosion sculpted these beautiful sandstone swirls in Utah.

people, turned to stone by the mythical trickster Coyote.

Working
with weather

Technology has changed the ways that we watch and predict weather. We can track weather and issue warnings better than ever before. This radar picture shows moisture within a hurricane. The red areas show where the most rain is, around the eye.

Weather watching

Every day, more than 10,000 weather stations on land and at sea are monitoring weather and climate and sending information to meteorologists and forecasters.

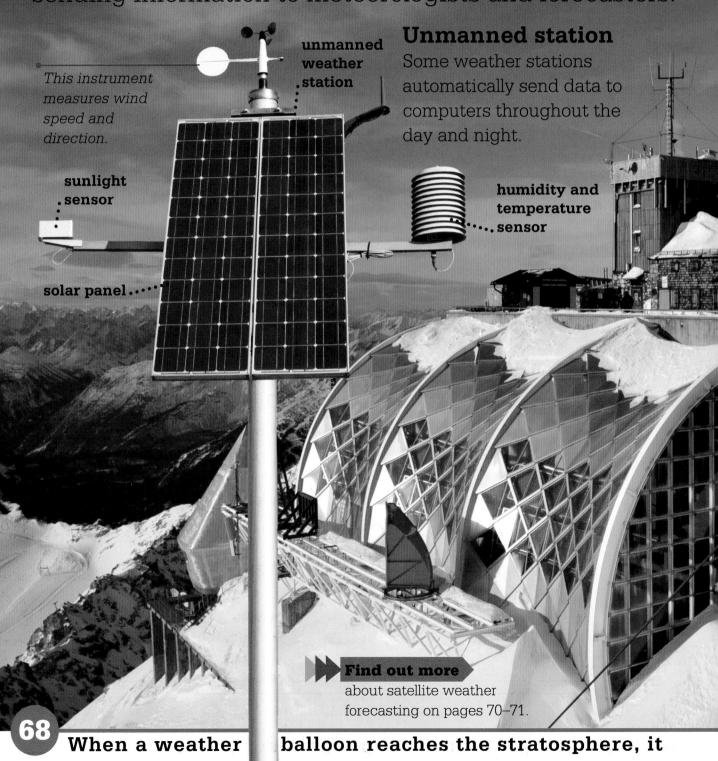

This instrument measures wind speed and direction.

unmanned weather station

sunlight sensor

solar panel

Unmanned station

Some weather stations automatically send data to computers throughout the day and night.

humidity and temperature sensor

▶▶ **Find out more** about satellite weather forecasting on pages 70–71.

When a weather balloon reaches the stratosphere, it

Mountain station

There are weather stations staffed by scientists in all climates, all over the world. This one is on the highest mountain in Germany.

Münchner Haus weather station

Weather balloon

Weather balloons fly up to the stratosphere, carrying instruments to measure pressure, temperature, and humidity.

Radar dish

Radar dishes use radio waves to detect rain, snow, and hail in the air. The information is converted into images on maps, like the one on pages 66–67.

bursts, and a parachute drops the instruments down.

Eye in the sky

High up in space, weather satellites are constantly monitoring Earth from altitudes of 22,000 miles (35,000 km). They carry radiometers that scan Earth to form images.

Two types

Weather satellites are either geostationary (always hovering above the same point on Earth) or polar orbiting (moving from pole to pole).

Satellite data

In addition to creating images of land, sea, and clouds, satellites monitor temperature and moisture in the air. This gives us information on climate change and can help predict future weather patterns.

Weather forecasts

The information gathered from stations and satellites is studied by meteorologists. It is turned into forecasts, which can warn of dangerous approaching weather.

Satellites are blasted toward space on rockets, then released to orbit Earth.

We can forecast only up to two weeks into the future.

The Aeolus satellite, to be launched in 2013, will track global wind patterns.

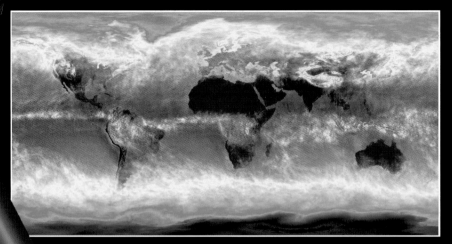

Snow-covered UK

Infrared satellite image

This global temperature satellite map shows 104°F (40°C) as dark red, down to –40°F (–40°C) as purple. Can you find the hot deserts and the cold polar seas?

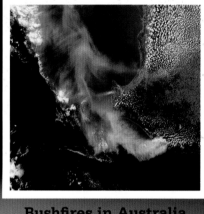

Bushfires in Australia

1025
H
1024
L 1005
1012

A blue line shows the leading edge of a cold front (a cold air mass).

A red line shows the leading edge of a warm front (a warm air mass).

A purple line shows where cold and warm fronts meet. This is called an occluded front. The weather is changeable here.

Dust storm in Alaska

Who knows what the weather will do after that?

Global warming

Scientists think that Earth is getting warmer—and we humans are to blame. A warmer planet means harmful changes to our weather.

Greenhouse gases

Our atmosphere contains greenhouse gases, which act like a blanket around Earth. They absorb and re-emit the Sun's heat, controlling Earth's temperature.

Burning oil to make electricity also creates CO_2.

Carbon dioxide

Carbon dioxide, or CO_2, is one of the greenhouse gases. Many experts think that humans produce too much CO_2, which is making our greenhouse blanket thicker.

Fumes from fuel engines in our cars contain CO_2.

We call these changes to our planet climate change.

Global warming

A thicker greenhouse blanket means that Earth traps more heat. As a result, Earth grows warmer. This phenomenon is called global warming.

Getting warmer

5.4–7.2°F
(3–4°C)
increase in temperature

3.6–5.4°F
(2–3°C)
increase in temperature

1.8–3.6°F
(1–2°C)
increase in temperature

0–1.8°F
(0–1°C)
increase in temperature

If Earth gets hotter

More hurricanes
Much warmer air may bring stormier weather and bigger hurricanes that sweep across the oceans.

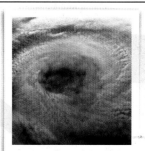

More droughts
As Earth warms, average temperatures may increase, bringing droughts to some areas.

More flooding
Hotter air means more water evaporation, and therefore more rain. Many more areas will flood.

Ice melt
Polar sea ice may melt, making the oceans rise. Some land may be covered with water.

We must try to keep Earth from warming up.

Saving our planet

To cut down on CO_2 emissions, we need to make small changes in our lives. The weather can help us, too!

These solar panels absorb the Sun's heat and turn it into electricity.

Use the weather

Burning coal and oil for electricity creates harmful carbon dioxide, or CO_2. Instead, we can use wind and the Sun's heat to make electricity.

A Xingu boy in Brazil grows new trees after the rainforest around him has been cut down.

Save the rainforests!

Trees naturally soak up harmful gases like CO_2. A huge amount of rainforest is cut down every day. This must be stopped so that the trees can continue to absorb CO_2.

Plant more trees

We need to replant trees as fast as we cut them down.

Give the car a break. Walk, bike, or ride a scooter to

What can you do at home?

1 Reduce, reuse, recycle!

It takes electricity to make products, so use fewer and recycle more.

2 Turn off lights

If you use less electricity, you will reduce the need for power stations to burn harmful fuels.

3 Buy local

Buy local food. The farther your food travels, the more fuel is used and the more CO_2 is released.

4 Spread the word

Research and prepare a save-the-planet project and present it to your class.

school to decrease exhaust fumes.

Glossary

air pressure
The weight of Earth's atmosphere pressing down on everything below it. High air pressure generally brings clear weather; low air pressure generally brings wet weather.

atmosphere
The layers of gases that surround a planet or star. The air is Earth's atmosphere.

aurora
A dazzling display of lights in the atmosphere, seen near the North and South Poles.

Beaufort scale
The scale used to measure the force of wind. It ranges from 0 (calm) to 12 (hurricane).

bushfire
A wildfire that occurs in the trees and bushes of dry scrublands or forests.

climate
The long-term or average weather in a particular area.

cloud
A mass of water droplets and ice crystals that is visible in the sky. Rain, snow, and hail fall from clouds.

cold front
The edge of an incoming mass of cold air.

condense
To turn from a gas into a liquid or solid. Water vapor condenses to become water and ice.

dense
Tightly packed. Cold air is denser than hot air is, so it exerts higher pressure.

drought
An unusually long period during which little or no rain falls. Droughts can cause vegetation to die.

erode
To break down or wear away. Wind, water, and ice erode rock and other surfaces.

evaporate
To turn from a liquid into a gas. Heat from the Sun makes water evaporate into the air.

global warming
The warming of Earth's atmosphere, thought to lead to climate change, and probably caused by greenhouse gases that include carbon dioxide.

lenticular
Shaped like a lens— that is, round and flat.

meteorologist
A scientist who studies the atmosphere, including weather and climate.

monsoon

A strong wind that changes direction according to the season. Monsoons can bring torrential rain from the sea.

occluded front

The meeting place of a cold front and a warm front. A thunderstorm or even a hurricane may occur here.

precipitation

Water that falls from the atmosphere to the ground as rain, snow, or hail.

rime ice

Ice created by fog or water vapor that has cooled and frozen onto a surface.

satellite

A spacecraft that orbits Earth. Weather satellites transmit information about conditions in the atmosphere back to the ground.

Snowflakes can range from almost invisible to up to 2 in. (5 cm) across.

storm surge

An abnormal rise in sea level along a coast, caused by a storm. This rise may result in flooding.

warm front

The edge of an incoming mass of warm air.

water vapor

Water in its gas form. The atmosphere contains water vapor.

weather

The condition of the atmosphere. For example, the weather may be hot, cold, rainy, sunny, snowy, or windy. Weather is created by air pressure, temperature, water, and the movement of air.

whiteout

A condition of intense snow that makes it difficult to see anything.

wind

The movement of air. Winds occur when warm air rises and cooler air moves to take its place.

Index

*A lightning flash may
be 3 miles (5 km) long
but only about a third
of an inch (1 cm) wide.*